FLOORED! SUPERCARS

CORVETTE

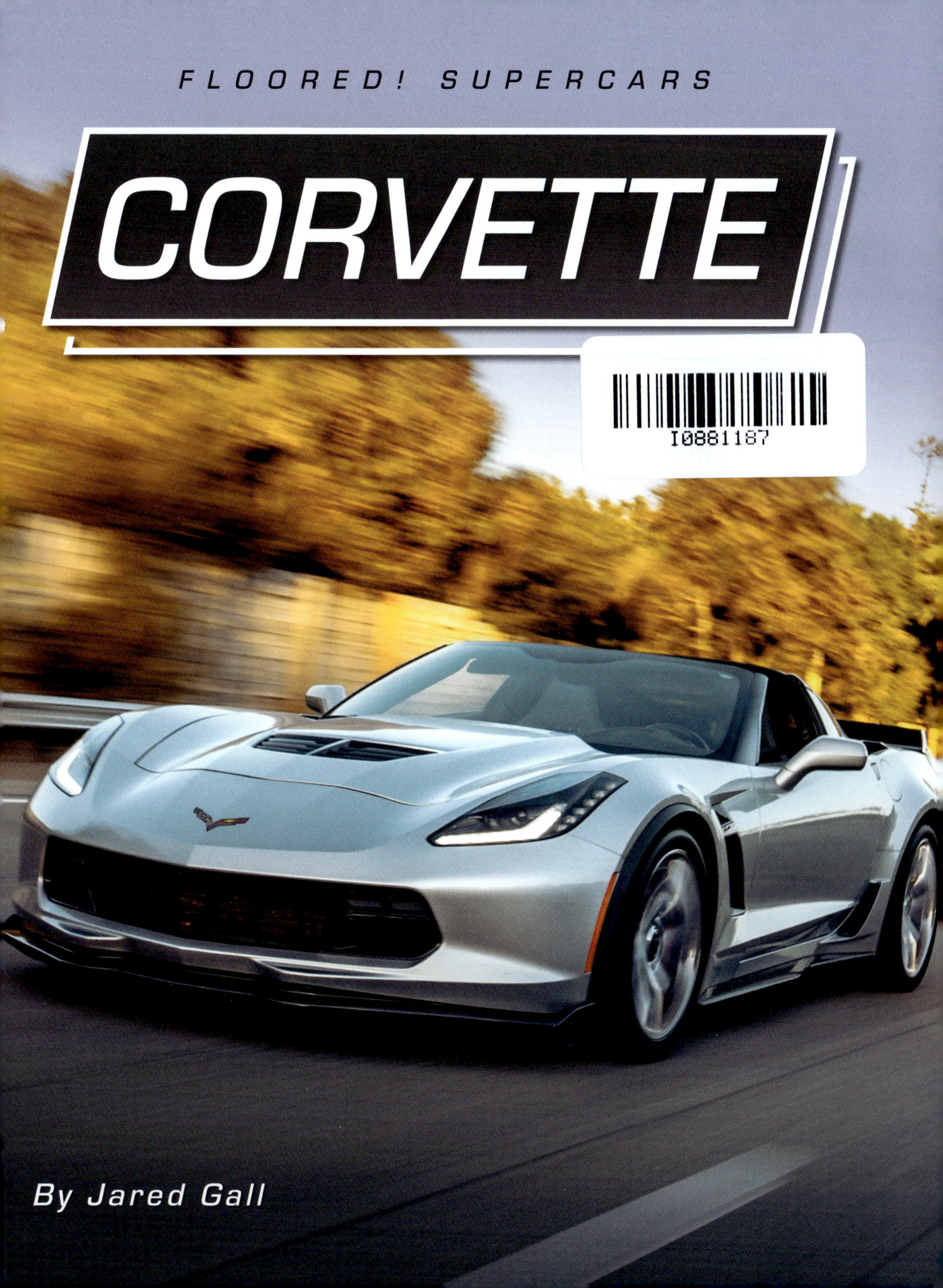

By Jared Gall

45TH PARALLEL PRESS

Published in the United States of America by Cherry Lake Publishing Group
Ann Arbor, Michigan
www.cherrylakepublishing.com

Reading Adviser: Beth Walker Gambro, MS, Ed., Reading Consultant, Yorkville, IL

Photo Credits: © ryan_photographs1/iStock, cover, title page; © Sam Kal/Shutterstock, 3; © Ethan Yetman/Shutterstock, 4; © Brandon Woyshnis/Shutterstock, 6–7; © Matt Fowler KC/Shutterstock, 8; David Wayne Buck/Shutterstock, 10 (left); © NeydtStock/Shutterstock, 10 (right); Unknown author, Public domain, via Wikimedia Commons, 11; © The Image Engine/Shutterstock, 12–13; Courtesy of National Corvette Museum Library & Archives, 14 (top & bottom); © Eric Glenn/Shutterstock, 16; © The Image Engine/Shutterstock, 18–19; © Jens Mommens/Shutterstock, 20; © Gabo_Arts/Shutterstock, 22–23; © Gabo_Arts/Shutterstock, 24; © quiggyt4/Shutterstock, 26; © Jack Skeens/Shutterstock, 28–29; © The Image Engine/Shutterstock, 30 (top); © chrisjj/Shutterstock, 30 (bottom); © Darren Brode/Shutterstock, 31 (top); © Brandon Woyshnis/Shutterstock, 31 (bottom)

45th Parallel Press is an imprint of Cherry Lake Publishing Group.

Library of Congress Cataloging-in-Publication Data

Names: Gall, Jared, author.
Title: Corvette / by Jared Gall.
Description: Ann Arbor, Michigan : 45th Parallel Press, 2025. | Series: Floored! Supercars | Includes bibliographical references. | Audience: Grades 4-6 | Summary: "Tech and innovation are at the forefront of luxury supercars. This book explores the cool features that make Corvettes some of the best high-performance vehicles in the world. From the history of the brand, to fast facts, and awesome photos--these books have enough to keep any car enthusiast engaged. This high-interest series is written at a low readability to aid struggling readers. Books feature educational sidebars, table of contents, glossary, index, author biography, and timeline"-- Provided by publisher.
Identifiers: LCCN 2024035967 | ISBN 9781668956618 (hardcover) | ISBN 9781668957462 (paperback) | ISBN 9781668958339 (ebook) | ISBN 9781668959206 (pdf)
Subjects: LCSH: Corvette automobile--History--Juvenile literature. | Corvette automobile--Design and construction--Juvenile literature.
Classification: LCC TL215.C6 G349 2025 | DDC 629.222/2--dc23/eng/20240923
LC record available at https://lccn.loc.gov/2024035967

Printed in the United States of America

Note from Publisher: Websites change regularly, and their future contents are outside of our control. Supervise children when conducting any recommended online searches for extended learning opportunities.

ABOUT THE AUTHOR:

Jared Gall writes about cars and trucks for magazines and websites. He has driven everything from semitrucks and school buses to sports cars and supercars. He has raced off-road buggies through the desert in Mexico and Mercedes-Benzes on frozen lakes in Sweden. He has driven a lot of Mercedes-Benzes, but never an AMG One. His personal top speed is 189 miles (304.2 kilometers) per hour, set while driving a Ferrari.

Table of Contents

A C8 Corvette Stingray. This Corvette model has been made since 2020.

CHAPTER 1

Introduction

There are many kinds of cars. They're good at different things. Minivans have lots of space. Whole families can fit. They can ride together to school. They can ride together on vacation. **Sport utility vehicles** are called SUVs. They also have lots of space. They're made to tow heavy things. They tow boats. They tow campers. They also go off-roading.

Sports cars are built to be fast. They're fun to drive. They're small. They're light. This makes them **agile**. Agile means they can turn quickly and easily. They go around corners fast.

Supercars are like sports cars. But they go even faster. Their engines have more power. They're lighter. They go faster on straight roads. They turn faster. Many are built with special metal. This makes them extra light.

Most supercars sit low. They're close to the ground. This makes them **aerodynamic**. That means they move through air easily. Imagine putting your hand out a car window. Imagine facing your palm into the wind. It would be hard to keep your hand still. But what if you lay your hand flat? It would then be

easier to hold your hand steady. Your hand is more aerodynamic when it's flat. Being aerodynamic makes supercars fast.

Have you ever seen a Corvette? Have you seen one on the road? If so, then you have seen a supercar! Corvettes are special. Let's learn more!

Corvettes made in 1953 are extra special. Each one was painted white. They were red inside. They're fun to collect.

CHAPTER 2

Corvette History

Chevrolet is known as Chevy. It's a U.S. car company. It started making cars in 1911. In the 1950s, it wanted to build a new car. The company wanted it to be exciting.

At that time, small **roadsters** were popular. They didn't have roofs. Roadsters have 2 seats.

Chevy wanted its own roadster. It was called the Corvette. It's named after a battleship. Corvettes are small ships. They're the smallest warships. They're fast. They're used as missile boats. They're used to make fast attacks.

Imagine a car version of these warships. Chevy Corvettes move easily. They turn fast.

Chevy wanted to race the Corvette. The company created a fun logo for the car. It was 2 crossed flags. One is a **checkered** flag. Checkered means a pattern of squares. The squares have different colors. Checkered flags are waved at car races. This happens at the end of a race. A checkered flag means victory.

The logo has changed a bit over time. But old and new have a red flag. The Chevy symbol is on the red flag.

The old and new logos also have a **fleur-de-lis**. It is a French symbol. It looks like a lily. Two of Chevy's founders were Louis and Arthur Chevrolet. They were from France.

The modern Chevy symbol (right) looks like a bow tie. It represents strength. It represents luxury.

Chevrolet was founded in 1911 by Louis Chevrolet (pictured here), Arthur Chevrolet, and William C. Durant.

Chevy started selling Corvettes in 1953. It built the first ones by hand. It made the body out of **fiberglass**. Fiberglass is a kind of plastic that is reinforced with glass. Most cars were made from steel. Fiberglass is lighter than steel. It's also easier to shape. Corvettes are still made of fiberglass today.

The first Corvettes weren't popular. Chevy built only 300 the first year. That's not a lot. Today, it sells more Corvettes than that each week.

Chevy wanted to give up. It almost quit making Corvettes. Then Ford started building a roadster. It was called the Thunderbird. Chevy wanted to beat Ford. It kept making Corvettes.

Chevy needed new ideas. It changed the leadership for the Corvette. This happened in 1955. Zora Arkus-Duntov became the leader. He was a racing driver. He was also an **engineer**. Engineers design things. They build things.

Arkus-Duntov improved Corvettes. He made them more powerful. He made them faster. He put in bigger engines. This made Corvettes more popular. They became the world's best-selling sports car. Arkus-Duntov saved the Corvette. He became known as "the father of the Corvette."

People could order cool wheel colors on the 1962 Corvette Roadster. Red was one of them.

Donna Mae Mims had a pink jumpsuit and a pink hat. She was proud to be a female race car driver.

Behind the Wheel

It's not as common for women to drive race cars. There are more male drivers. In the 1960s, women race car drivers were very rare. **Donna Mae Mims** was a driver. She won many races in her Corvette. She was known as the "Pink Lady" of racing. She painted "Think Pink" on her car. She wore a pink wig. She wore a pink helmet.

Mims and 2 other women entered a race. They did this in 1972. They drove a limo. A limo is a big, long car. It's built for comfort. Limos aren't like most race cars. This race was not like most races. This race was across the United States. It was not on a racetrack. It was on public roads. It went from New York to Los Angeles. Mims and her teammates did not finish. But a movie was based on that race... It was called *The Cannonball Run.*

A total of 10,594 split-window Corvette coupes were made in 1963. People collect them now.

CHAPTER 3

Corvette Evolution

Chevy redesigned the Corvette in 1963. The 1963 Corvette is called the C2. It's the second generation of the Corvette. Its rear window is 2 pieces of glass. It looked cool. But it was hard to see out the back. Chevy made the window 1 piece. This happened in 1964. Corvettes with the split rear window are rare today. That makes them valuable.

Corvette engines got bigger in the 1960s. They got more powerful. Chevy designed a racing Corvette. This happened in 1962. It was called the Grand Sport. Chevy wanted to build more than 100. But then the company stopped racing. Only 5 were built. Many companies today make Grand Sport **replicas**. A replica is a copy.

Corvettes have upgrade options. Z06 (zee oh six) and ZR1 are 2 options. Z06s are racing upgrades. ZR1s have the most powerful upgrades. The first ZR1 was a C3 Corvette.

The C3 Corvette came out in 1968. This was the first Corvette with a **T-top**. T-tops have 2 panels in the roof. These panels come off. This makes them look like **convertibles**. Convertibles have tops that fold down or come off. Corvettes no longer have T-tops. Now they have a single roof panel that comes off. This is called a **targa top**.

In the 1970s, things changed. The U.S. government made cars use different gas. This was to reduce **pollution**. Pollution is substances that harm the environment. The new gas made Corvette engines weaker.

The C4 came out in 1984. Chevy introduced the C4 ZR1 in 1990. This ZR1 was the fastest version of the Corvette. It cost more. Chevy took it to a racetrack in Texas. This ZR1 set a world record. It drove faster than 175 miles (282 kilometers) per hour. It did this for 24 hours straight.

What Corvettes in the 1970s lacked in engine power they made up for in style.

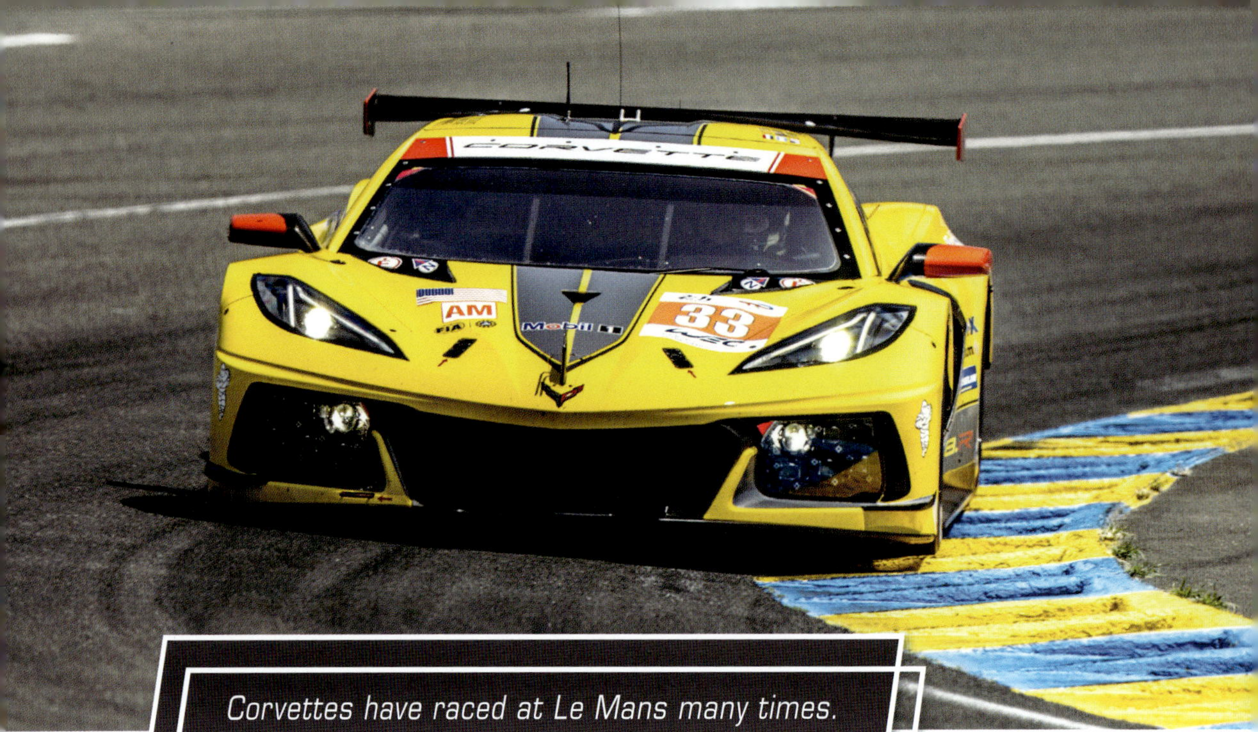

Corvettes have raced at Le Mans many times. They've won first place. They did this 9 times.

Chevy added the Z06 upgrades on the C5 Corvette. The Z06 version had a faster engine. It had better brakes. It was another faster version of the Corvette. It's not as fast as Corvettes with the ZR1 upgrades. Chevy decided to start racing again. The C5 Corvette won many famous races.

The American Le Mans Series was a series of races. It took place in the United States. It was like the 24 Hours of Le Mans. It starts in the afternoon on a Saturday. It ends 24 hours later, in the afternoon on Sunday. Teams of drivers take turns driving, eating, and sleeping. C5 Corvettes raced at Le Mans 5 times. They won 3 times. That's a very good record.

Fast Facts

- The Corvette Sting Ray came out in 1963. In 1969, it was called one word: Stingray.
- The most valuable Corvette ever was a C3. Its engine was called the L88. One sold for almost $4 million. This happened in 2014.
- Corvettes are built in Bowling Green, Kentucky. Visitors can tour the factory. A museum is next to the factory. It has many unique Corvettes.
- There's a cave under the National Corvette Museum. In 2014, it collapsed. A giant hole opened up. The hole was in the middle of the museum. Eight Corvettes fell in. Three were fixed. The other 5 are back in the museum. But they're still damaged.
- There was no 1983 Corvette. Chevy had stopped building the 1982 car. But the new model wasn't quite ready.

The C6 Corvette came out in 2005. It was a hit.

The American Le Mans Series is a series of races. It takes place in the United States. It's like the 24 Hours of Le Mans. Some of the races were 12 hours long. Others were 24 hours. Corvettes won 25 races in a row. They did this from 2007 to 2009. They have the longest winning streak.

The C7 Corvette Z06 was Chevy's most powerful car at the time. It first came out in 2014. Then Chevy made a new C7 ZR1. It did this in 2018. The ZR1 was more powerful than the Z06. But it wasn't much faster than the Z06. It was time for a big change.

A C7 Corvette ZR1

Most convertibles have cloth tops. The C8 Corvette has a metal roof. The roof folds and tucks behind the driver.

CHAPTER 4

Corvette Today

The C8 is the first **mid-engine** Corvette. Engines are in the front of most cars. In mid-engine cars, engines are in the middle. They're behind the driver. Most supercars are mid-engines. Putting the engine in the middle makes cars easier to drive. It also makes them more aerodynamic.

Zora Arkus-Duntov wanted to make Corvettes mid-engine. Chevy did not agree. Arkus-Duntov built the first mid-engine Corvette **prototype**. He did this in 1960. Prototypes are models. They show how something could be done.

It's expensive to build mid-engine cars. The trunk in most cars is behind the driver. Putting the engine behind the driver doesn't leave much room for a trunk. So mid-engine cars tend to have small trunks.

The C8 Corvette has a small trunk. The trunk is at the front of the car. Some people combine *front* with *trunk*. A front trunk is a *frunk*.

Older Corvettes didn't look like supercars. The mid-engine Corvette does. Supercars cost a lot. Corvettes cost less than other supercars. But they're just as powerful.

The Corvette E-Ray is Chevy's hybrid Corvette.

Cost of Ownership

MODEL	PRICE
2024 Toyota Camry	$27,500
2024 Honda CR-V	$31,000
2024 Ford F-150	$39,000

MODEL	PRICE
2024 Chevrolet Corvette	$68,500
2024 Chevrolet Corvette convertible	$75,500
2024 Chevrolet Corvette E-Ray	$105,000
2024 Chevrolet Corvette E-Ray convertible	$112,000
2024 Chevrolet Corvette Z06	$112,500
2024 Chevrolet Corvette Z06 convertible	$117,000

Chevy's Z06 Corvette uses a special engine. The engines are like the ones in Corvette race cars. There are also **hybrid** Corvettes. Hybrid cars have gas engines and electric motors. This makes them more **efficient**. Efficient means not to waste energy. Efficient cars can go farther before needing to stop for gas.

The hybrid Corvette is called the E-Ray. It's more efficient than regular Corvettes. It's faster, too! Corvettes built before the E-Ray have **rear-wheel drive**. This means the rear wheels power the car to make it go. In E-Rays, gas engines turn the rear wheels. Electric motors turn the front wheels. This makes E-Rays **all-wheel drive** cars. All 4 wheels power the car.

Chevy isn't done making the C8 Corvette faster. The new ZR1 has 1,064 horsepower. It can go faster than 215 miles (346 km) per hour. And Chevy will build even more powerful hybrids in the future. They'll be the fastest Corvettes ever.

Corvettes are a symbol of American power. They're a top American sports car. They're known for their speed. They're known for their performance. They're in movies. They're mentioned in songs. They're driven by famous people. They're one of the most popular cars ever made. What do you think the future of the Corvette will look like?

Experts estimate the C8 ZR1 can go a quarter mile (.4 km) in under 10 seconds.

Timeline of a Legend

1953

- C1 is the first Corvette produced.

1955

- Ford Thunderbird comes out. Chevy wants to compete. It keeps making the Corvette.

1960

- Zora Arkus-Duntov builds the first mid-engine Corvette prototype.

1963

- C2 is introduced.

1967

- C3 is introduced.

1984

C4 production starts.

1986

Chevy builds another mid-engine Corvette prototype.

1990

First C4 ZR1 is produced.

2001

First C5 Z06 is introduced.

2014

C7 debuts.

2020

Mid-engine C8 Corvette is introduced.

Find Out More

BOOKS

Magnante, Steve. *Steve Magnante's 1001 Corvette Facts*. North Branch, MN: CarTech, 2018.

Mueller, Mike. *The Complete Book of Corvette*. Beverly, MA: Motorbooks, 2020.

WEBSITES

Search these online sources with an adult:

Corvette Facts for Kids | Kiddle

About Corvette | National Corvette Museum

Glossary

24 Hours of Le Mans (twen-tee-FOR OW-uhrz uhv luh MAHNZ) a famous endurance race in France

aerodynamic (air-oh-dye-NA-mik) able to move easily through the air

agile (A-juhl) able to change direction quickly

all-wheel drive (AWL WEEL DRYEV) a driving system that powers all 4 wheels of a vehicle

checkered (CHEH-kuhrd) covered with a pattern of squares

convertibles (kuhn-VUHR-tuh-buhlz) cars with tops that can be lowered or removed

efficient (ih-FIH-shuhnt) able to be more productive with less energy

engineer (en-juh-NEER) a person who designs and builds things

fiberglass (FYE-ber-glaas) a structural material made of glass fibers and plastic

fleur-de-lis (flur-duh-LEE) a French symbol that looks like a lily

hybrid (HYE-bruhd) a car with a gasoline engine and an electric motor

mid-engine (mid-EN-juhn) having the engine behind the driver

pollution (puh-LOO-shuhn) things such as chemicals and waste that harm the environment

prototype (PROH-tuh-TYEP) an original model of something that shows how it will work

rear-wheel drive (REER-weel DRYEV) a driving system that powers the back wheels of a vehicle

replicas (REH-plih-kuhz) exact copies of something that is often older

roadsters (ROHD-stuhrz) 2-seat cars without roofs

sport utility vehicles (SPORT yoo-TIH-luh-tee VEE-uh-kuhlz) vehicles designed to be used on rough surfaces but often used on city streets; also called SUVs

supercars (SOO-puhr-kahrz) cars designed to go faster than other cars

targa top (TAR-guh TAHP) a car roof with 1 removable panel

T-top (TEE-tahp) a car roof with 2 removable panels

Index